Found in a River

Steelhead & Other Revelations

Found in a River

Steelhead & Other Revelations

Jeff Bright

words, photography & design

Frank Amato
PORTLAND

Gratitude

Dedicated to the memory of my grandfathers, Charley Urmey and Paul Bright, fine men and fine fishermen. Thank you both for leading me to the water's edge. And dedicated to Scott Ellsworth for pushing me in.

Special thanks to Clair for her loving indulgence, encouragement and the most delicious brown bag lunches a fisherman could hope for.

The author would also like to  acknowledge Michael Fong, without whose help this book may not have been published. Michael passed away unexpectedly June 14, 2002. The flyfishing community will miss one of its shining lights. Thank you, Mike.

Published in 2002 by Frank Amato Publications, Inc.
P.O. Box 82112, Portland, Oregon 97282
(503) 653-8108 • www.amatobooks.com

Hardbound ISBN: 1-57188-282-0 • Hardbound UPC: 0-66066-00515-1

All photographs taken by author except where noted.
Book Design: Jeff Bright

Printed in Singapore
1 3 5 7 9 10 8 6 4 2

Contents

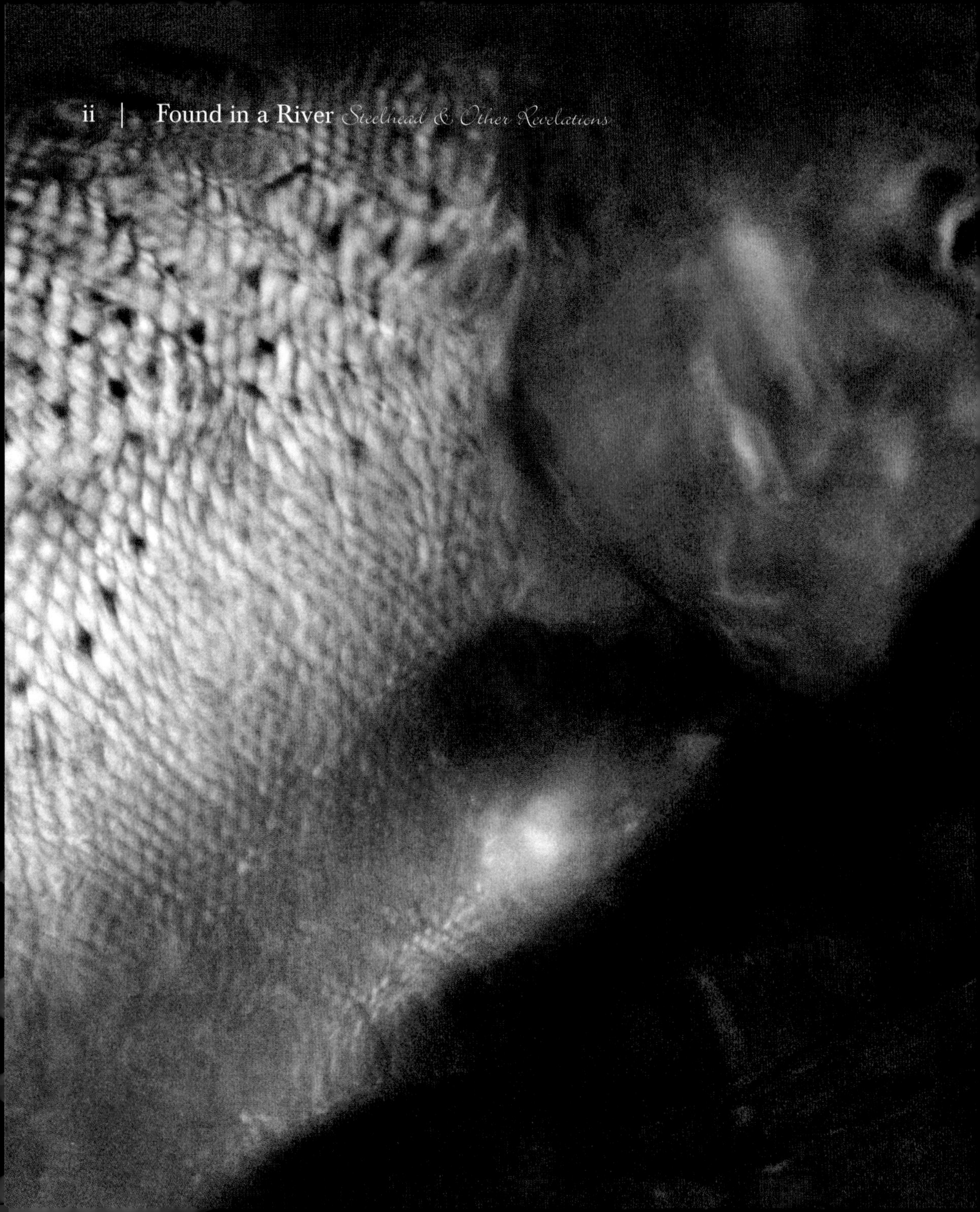

Prologue

On a sun-shot day in January of 1994 a good friend introduced me to the world of steelhead fishing on a small coastal stream in Northern California. The day unfolded like a dream. In short, with borrowed, mismatched gear and an ample dose of beginner's luck, I caught a good fish – a heavy male in full spawning color. A fierce, strong and wild force that nearly yanked my arms from their sockets. The experience was a powerful one. One that, at the time, I needed more than I knew and that lit in me a fire of obsession.

I was born and raised in Ohio and and my early fishing took place on Michigan's Upper Peninsula. I had fished and caught big fish before. Bass, northern pike, walleye and musky. But this was different. This fish seemed to get inside me. This ocean voyager and royalty of western rivers. This steelhead. I had to know more.

I made the three-hour trip back to that same river and pool from my San Francisco apartment numerous times that winter and in the several ensuing winters. I caught more steelhead. I lost more than I caught. I suffered through broken leaders, broken rods, exploding reels and straightened hooks – among other maladies. I fell down and I fell in. I got soaked and I got stung. I got lost in the dark and bitten by ticks. On one odiously memorable occasion I was lifted from my footing while attempting to cross a swift tailout and escorted around a bend into a stand of willow sweepers against a high bank. Fortunately the river was not a generally deep river and I was eventually able to disentangle myself from the branches and make my way to shore, sloshing, sputtering and dripping, grabbing the assorted contents of my vest as they floated by. I emerged with a good deal of humility, a newfound respect for the force of flowing water and a lesson I won't soon forget.

Over the next few years I made countless trips up and down the California coast. Highways 1 and 101 and Interstate 5 became second homes. I wore out my Jeep Cherokee on Highway 299, chasing rumors of fish from one end of the Trinity River to the other. From the dam at Lewiston to the confluence with the Klamath at Weitchpec, I flogged the water and dreamed of steelhead.

I caught my first steelhead on a fly on a peculiarly dark morning in August of 1997 on the Trinity. The previous September a guide on Vancouver Island's Campbell River had given me the fly, a simple variation on a Del Cooper. It was a plain but clownish looking red, white and purple number. Its hook had been sharpened so many times I laughed to myself as I tried to fashion a point on the remaining knuckle. I doubted it would even stick in the unlikely event a fish should strike. I didn't think I'd have to worry about it…I'd heard that pursuing steelhead on a fly was an exercise in futility.

But hope is an avaricious sprite. It has a way of tricking even the most guarded cynic into doing things they figured they'd never do. And all fishers, regardless of their chosen methods, must carry at least an ounce of hope with them when they set out to go fishing – it's our common bond. So with the faintest glimmer of this sneaky hope, I tied the fly on the end of my leader and cast it into the early morning fog.

Lo and behold! A miracle occurred. The rod bucked. The reel whirred. Line melted off the spool – and I did have to worry about that sorry hook.

The fish was not particularly large, maybe four pounds. A mysterious and surprising remnant of the river's mainstem summer run. Still, I was jazzed. My mind roared a thousand exclamations and I knew there was no turning back. I had just been given a tantalizing taste of one of flyfishing's sweetest nectars – *steelhead on a fly*. From that point on, I vowed, I'd raise the bar. I'd use nothing but flies in my steelhead angling. I knew my catch rate would plummet and the learning curve would be steep and slippery. I was giving up a sure thing for the dark unknown. I'd spent a small fortune on conventional rods, reels and gear and winced at the thought of it all collecting dust. But once again I was smitten. The experience was too exciting, intriguing and challenging – the connection so vitally direct – not to make the commitment.

Though many have attempted to describe in words the thrill of catching a steelhead fresh from the sea on a fly, I'm sure that none would say they have done the event justice. Flyfishing for steelhead is more than a bit masochistic. Hour upon aching hour without even a tug. Cast after unanswered cast. Days, weeks and months can pile up fishless and frustrating.

Then it happens. Sudden and unexpected. The fish is on and running. Your reel sings a mechanical opera. Your flyrod is transmitting a wild and electric pulse up your arms and into your spine. Your cortex hums and crackles with the encoded mysteries of the ocean. Evolutionary secrets are being divulged – if only you could decipher them. The fish jumps. It jumps again, and a third time, high over your head. You check its surges and regain the line. Several times. You follow down the bank and finally the fish is lying in the shallows. You grip it around the wrist of its tail, unhook the fly and hold it gently in the water. You try to memorize its appearance…so many striking details…your mind is rushing…you may not see another for a long time…you wonder where it has been and what it has seen. You try to soak it all in, try to imprint the experience.

You take a few photos, hoping to capture the brilliant shifting prismatic colors, the radiance, the depth and and play of light on the fish's gill plates and flank, the translucence of the fins, the mystery in its eye, the heart-warming speckles that dot its back, the impossible whiteness of its belly. You hope the very spirit of the creature will miraculously ignore the mechanical limits of photography and dissolve into the film.

You cradle the fish, pointing it upstream in a lesser side current and move it slowly forward and back, inducing a flow of water through its gills. It makes a slow **S**-wriggle, then a solid purposeful bolt, breaking your grip. You watch as it disappears back into the center of the river's flow and marvel that such a sparkling gem out of water can appear so thoroughly camouflaged amidst the river stones. You finally exhale and offer a silent "bon voyage," hoping the fish is no worse off for participating and that it will spawn a profusion of hardy offspring.

Almost immediately you are at a loss to describe with any accuracy the details of what has just transpired. You can't get your arms around it. Something essential, some central piece of truth or understanding, has slipped away. You could talk about it all day and still never satisfactorily portray the event. And finally, you come to the undeniable realization – *you'll have to catch another!*

Perhaps this is why, knowing full well and good that it's going to be difficult, but possibly very fulfilling, we do it.

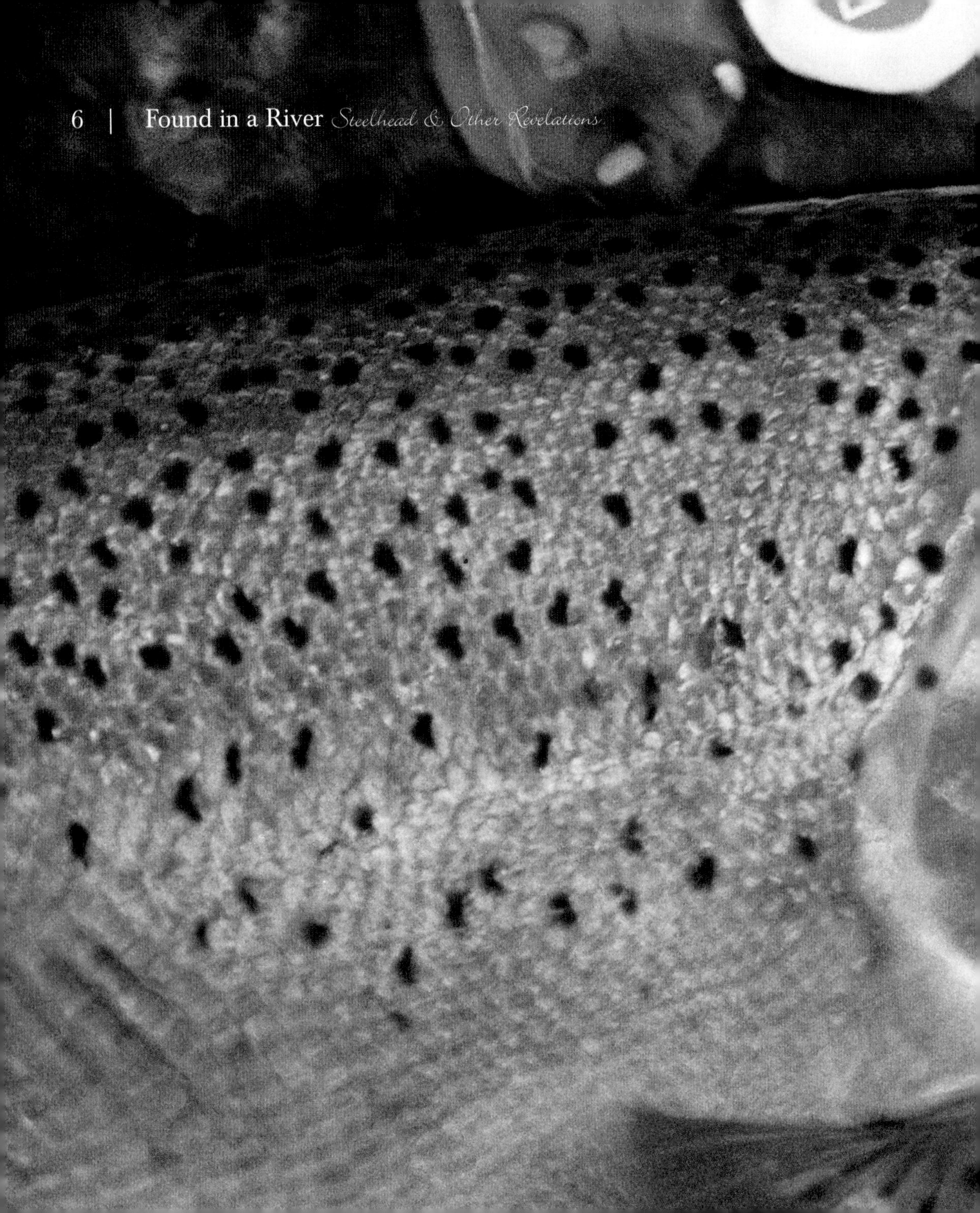

Iread every steelhead book I could get my hands on. The wise works of the master, Roderick Haig-Brown. The early California accounts of Claude Kreider and Clark Van Fleet. Ray Bergman's historic North Umpqua chapter in *Trout.* Jim Freeman's California Tackle Box series. Russell Chatham's significant and reverent North Coast chronicles. The pioneering works of Frank Amato and Ralph Wahl. Trey Combs' encyclopedic and epic work. The sensitive and passionate voices of Steve Raymond and Bob Arnold. The practical and indispensible books by John Shewey, Deke Meyer, Jed Davis and Bill Herzog. Fellow San Franciscan Michael Checchio's heady work. Tom McGuane and David James Duncan's incomparable literature. Bill McMillan's marvelous *Dry Line Steelhead,* which contains arguably the most valuable steelhead flyfishing writing ever committed to paper. And over and over I watched Lani Waller's exuberant and thrilling videotapes.

I sought out works peripheral to the steelhead angling genre, such as books by Jim Lichatowich and Freeman House. Both approach the appreciation and conservation of salmon and salmon bearing rivers from unique and essential perspectives. Both offer insights on how we might make cultural adjustments to allow the survival of the Northwest's anadromous fish.

(I'm happy to say, this is by no means a complete list. There are others to read, older books to find. As I write this, a just-acquired copy of Enos Bradner's Northwest Angling *is stacked at the ready with several classic Atlantic salmon titles and a few*

new works illuminating the growing Great Lakes steelhead fishery. I'm eager to pour over each sentence and paragraph, fact and opinion, drawing and photograph.)

I set a goal for myself to catch a steelhead in California in every month of the year. No easy feat since our summer runs have all but disappeared. I researched where there might be returning adult steelhead in a river in California on any given day of the year – or where they might have been 30 to 70 years ago when our ecosystems were in better health. In my research I began learning about the issues threatening the survival of steelhead and the wild places they need to thrive. I read and thought about how the survival of wilderness and the prosperity of the human spirit are intertwined. I ruminated on my experiences and awakenings and the personal value that steelhead and all our natural resources provide. I thought about responsibility, about stewardship, about morality.

To me it seemed the importance of the survival of our wild natural heritage was immense. How could we hope to exist with dignity, and maintain life worth the time it takes to live it, if we despoiled the place where we lived? If we altered the course of the natural process beyond its ability to sustain the life that ultimately must support us? I wondered if enough people actually understood the basic biological dynamic and the challenge that looms as human population expands and endangers the ability of natural resource supplies to meet demand? I wondered if people would care if they did understand? If after exposed to an informed argument would they agree that wilderness and the life that inhabits it has more value when it is alive and flourishing than when it is viewed through the crosshair of the marketplace?

I wondered who would agree or disagree that all citizens of the United States, by the intent of our laws, have a contract with each other – a contract that says in no uncertain terms: 1) that we are all entitled to and responsible for a healthy and functioning natural environment, 2) that air and water, the elements fundamental to life, belong to us all and cannot be co-opted for personal gain, and 3) that no person or entity has the right to foul those resources?

I wondered and wandered. And while I eventually met my personal angling goal, my eyes had been opened to the threats facing our already diminished steelhead populations. I was beset with waves of doom and dread. Steam rose in my heart.

I steered my graphic design business toward conservation organizations who were dealing with these issues, notably California Trout and Friends of the Trinity River. I began following the issues and documenting my fishing experiences. I took photographs and jotted down a note here and there. I began to think about how I could creatively address these issues and how I could apply my experiences and resources. I wanted to contribute on an ideological level. The result is this book.

Ultimately, the aim of *Found in a River* is to create value for wild steelhead and their rivers on an emotional, existential and experiential level. Its goal is to create sensitivity. It is my belief that if we are to enliven a new paradigm for the use and value of natural resources in our culture, especially in the West, we'll need to start on a very basic human level. The effort must be organic. We must weave our lives into the place, not the place into our lives. We must work from the ground up, from the heart and soul out.

Since my "steelhead satori" I've pursued these marvelous fish on rivers throughout Northern California, choosing to become intimate with a select few streams rather than loosely acquainted with many. I've also made brief forays to Oregon and to Vancouver Island in British Columbia – where staying at the Haig-Brown House, operated as a Canadian national heritage site and bed and breakfast, and fishing Haig-Brown's home water on the Campbell, was for me a trip to mecca.

My list of rivers fished is relatively short. But the rivers I have fished I have fished with fondness and a thirst for discovery, knowing there is much there to be learned. So it is with more than a fair amount of excitement that I think about the rivers I have yet to visit and the experiences waiting around each bend and in every riffle, pool and run.

When I am on a river now, I feel there is history taking place. A slow-moving and poignant pageant. A display that I am always grateful to witness. In this book I've attempted to make some account of that history and pageantry and how it has become meaningful for me. I've tried to convey how it has helped me to find some sense of place in the vast stream of time and how steelhead flyfishing has become my connection to the dense, unsolvable and magnetic mysteries that are the web of life.

Ancient Blood

I had been looking for a long time

When I found it in a river.

In the heathered belly of coastal hills and plains

Cutting through canyons steep and dark

Lying in valleys great and small

In the creases and folds of Northern California –

Ancient blood in a long-winded rhyme.

I followed the river

It hissing here, murmuring there

Wild, proud and free in one quadrant

Tamed and shamed, dirty and full of sorrow in another

Songs of joy and woe rolling through the rocks on its floor.

I observed distant and close its hinging moods –

Rampaging, crashing, silent, sparkling

Impatient, benevolent, by turns treacherous or teasing

Inviting, gentle, giving – then a crashing torrent of vengeance

Never apologizing. Never explaining.

I followed with childish faith

Through tangled brush and thickets of thorns

In swelter, storm and gale

Under glorious bluebird skies until

I could stand no more of the sun.

Beneath leering boulders, I ducked. Down crumbling cliffsides, I slid

Over cobbles worn smooth from rivertime witness, I stumbled

I was lured on and swallowed whole by the foggy-shrouded dawn

And beyond the crest of the day I rushed to be lost

In the creep of twilight and fish-lust.

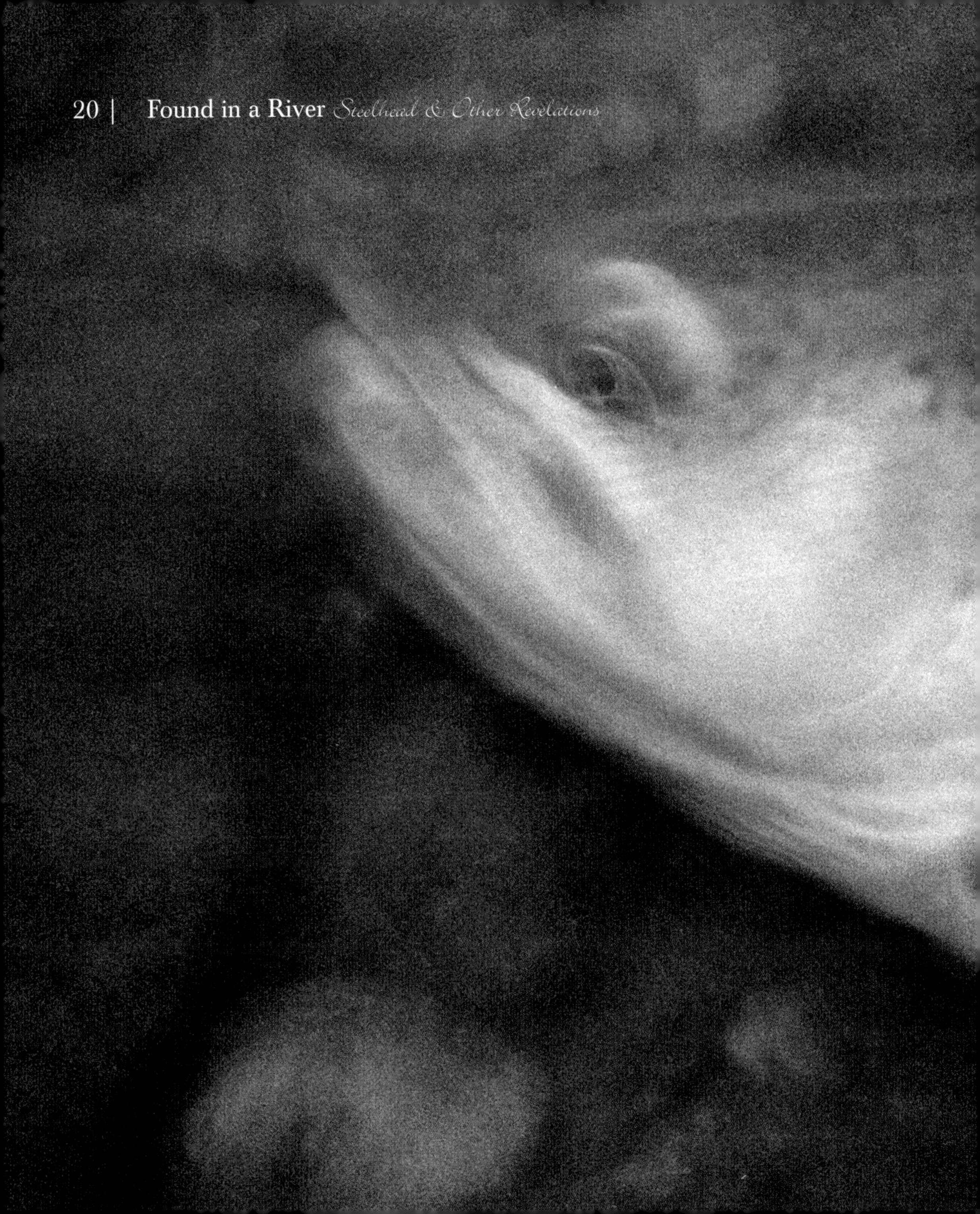

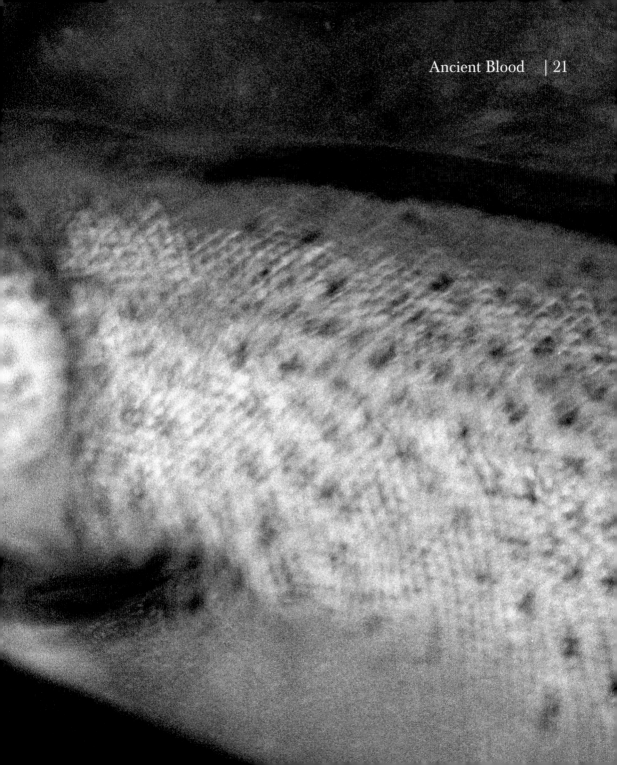

Some Distant Birdsong

I breathed in

As deep as I could the summer scent –

Bankside willows and blackberries ripening

A smothering sweat of mountain perfume

Lingering in solace for days otherwise fruitless.

I pined for autumn

Longing for the salmon to return

For them to die and rot and sting the air with their pungent end

To give themselves back to the river

To renew, nourish and relink the evermore tenuous chain.

But for winter I was most anxious

For its timid, slanting light and furtive vapors

For its shards of grey-white rain wind-whipped and riven from the sea

Wending like jewelry through boughs of redwood, fir and cedar

Trickling from my hat to my near-frozen nose…to the ferns…to the river.

Here I paused

Leaning into the current, waist-deep

Thoughts and concentrations thrumming

The alders behind me stark and austere, as if guarding secrets

The river streaming by in its emerald dress.

I stood at the edge of a notion

Time unravelling in a dense prehistoric ritual

Imperceptibly, among the gravel and stones at my feet

My breath rising and condensing in the chilled air

Then expiring into the surrounding mist.

I was transfixed –

Here was something of me, some evolutionary part

Some grain of knowledge carrying the wisdom for being

Some faint cadence being played in the mumbling stillness

Some distant birdsong that beckoned.

On into spring I gave chase

Following whispers and hunches and ghosts of dim ideas;

Coastal rivers receded to a polite stroll

Mountain rivers swelled and rushed with snowmelt

Hillsides conversed in a cacophony of California green.

I had been looking for new reasons to believe in a bedeviled world

When I found them in a river

Submerged in braided glides and swirling eddies

Deep in glassine pools – hidden from industry, absent from commerce

But revealed in glimpses to a curious and patient eye.

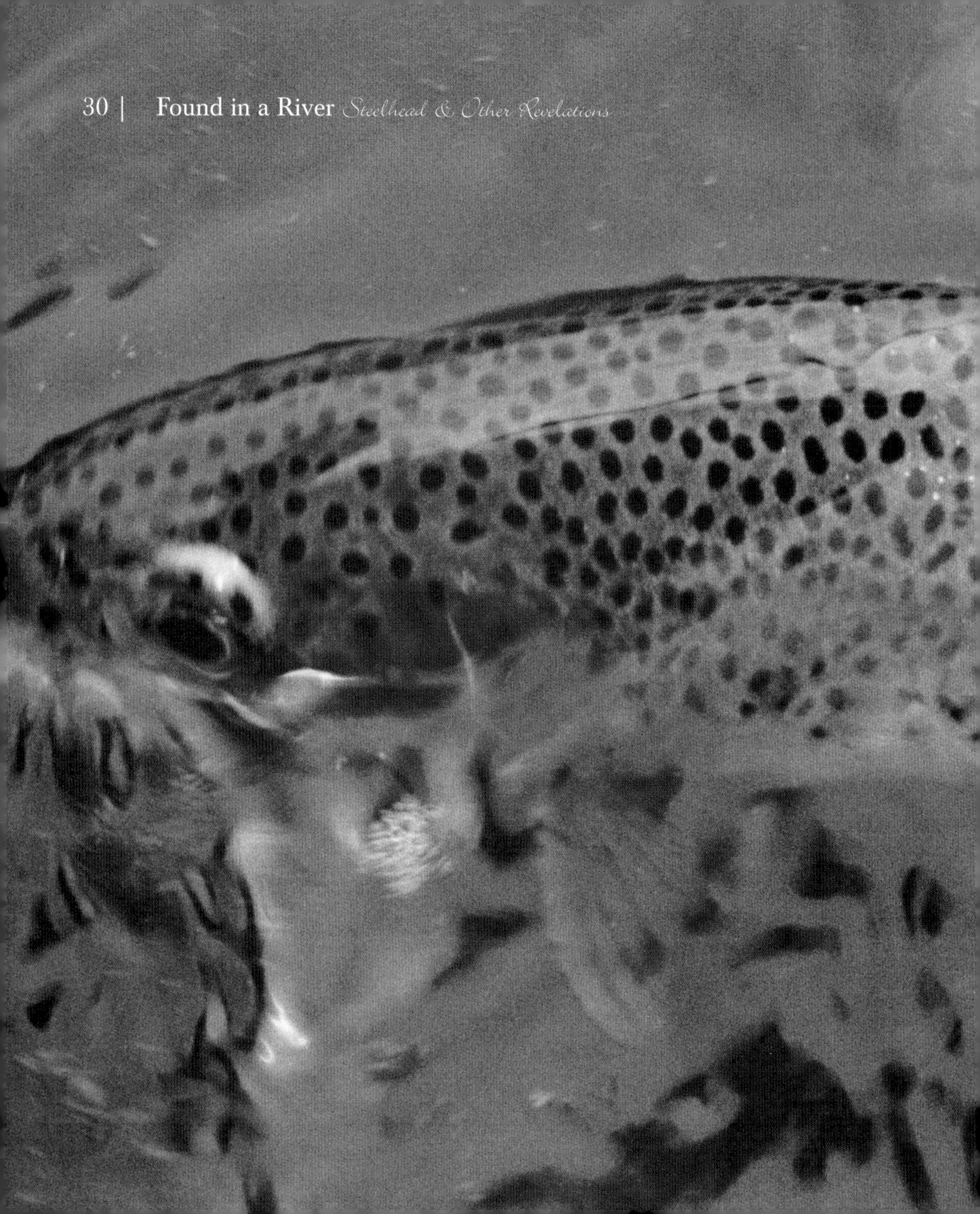

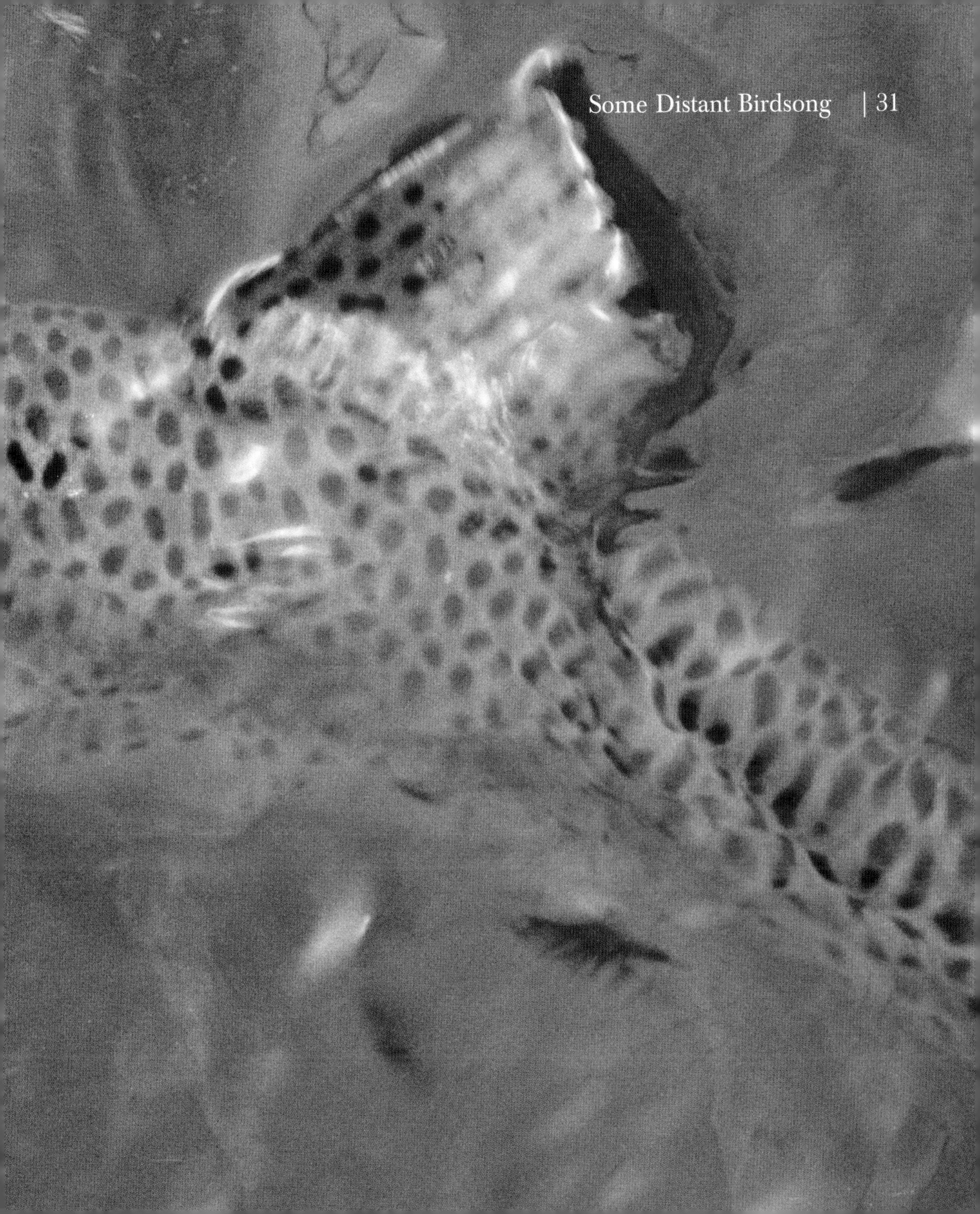

The Finest Trout

The river alone could have been enough

But in it I found a compelling saga

A form gem-like and polished

A life astonishing and epic in its history

– I found the finest trout that swims.

Born in the singing riffles

Pushed by the force of its life to the sea

Feasting and riding the current highways as far off as Japan

Then returning to the very river and pool of its conception

One survivor out of 10,000 siblings.

This is the steelhead trout

Shy, ghostly and elusive, secretive and aloof

Occasionally brazen and daring – even foolish

But always possessing a relentless will to survive

And a fierceness befitting the storm swells of the wild Pacific.

Lightning quick and acrobatic

Worthy of an angler's days spent in pursuit

In tidewaters, a shimmering vision of the ocean's silver-blue gleam

In headwaters, a carnival of colors – ripe red, pink-purple and luscious olive

I have been, and am still, *amazed.*

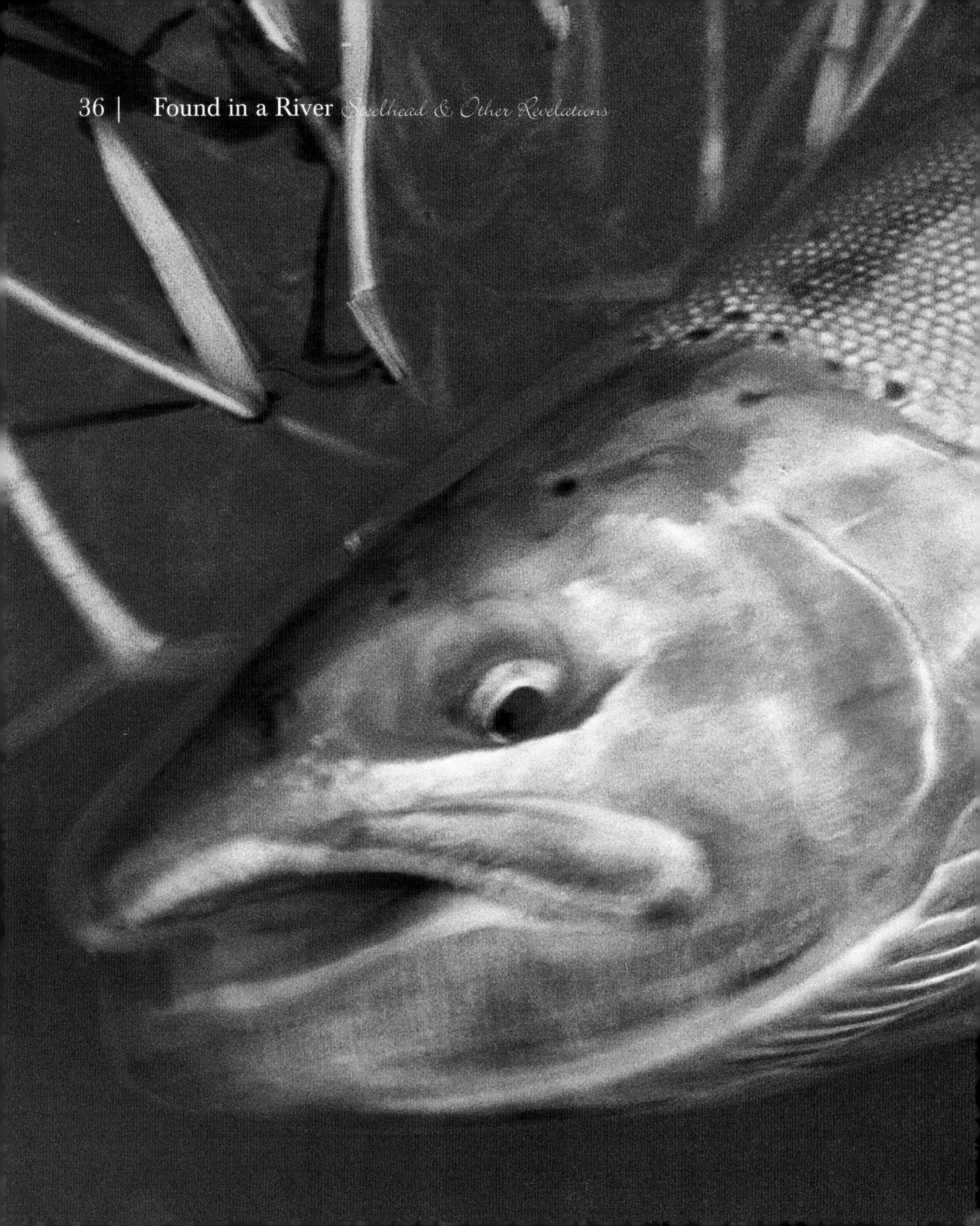

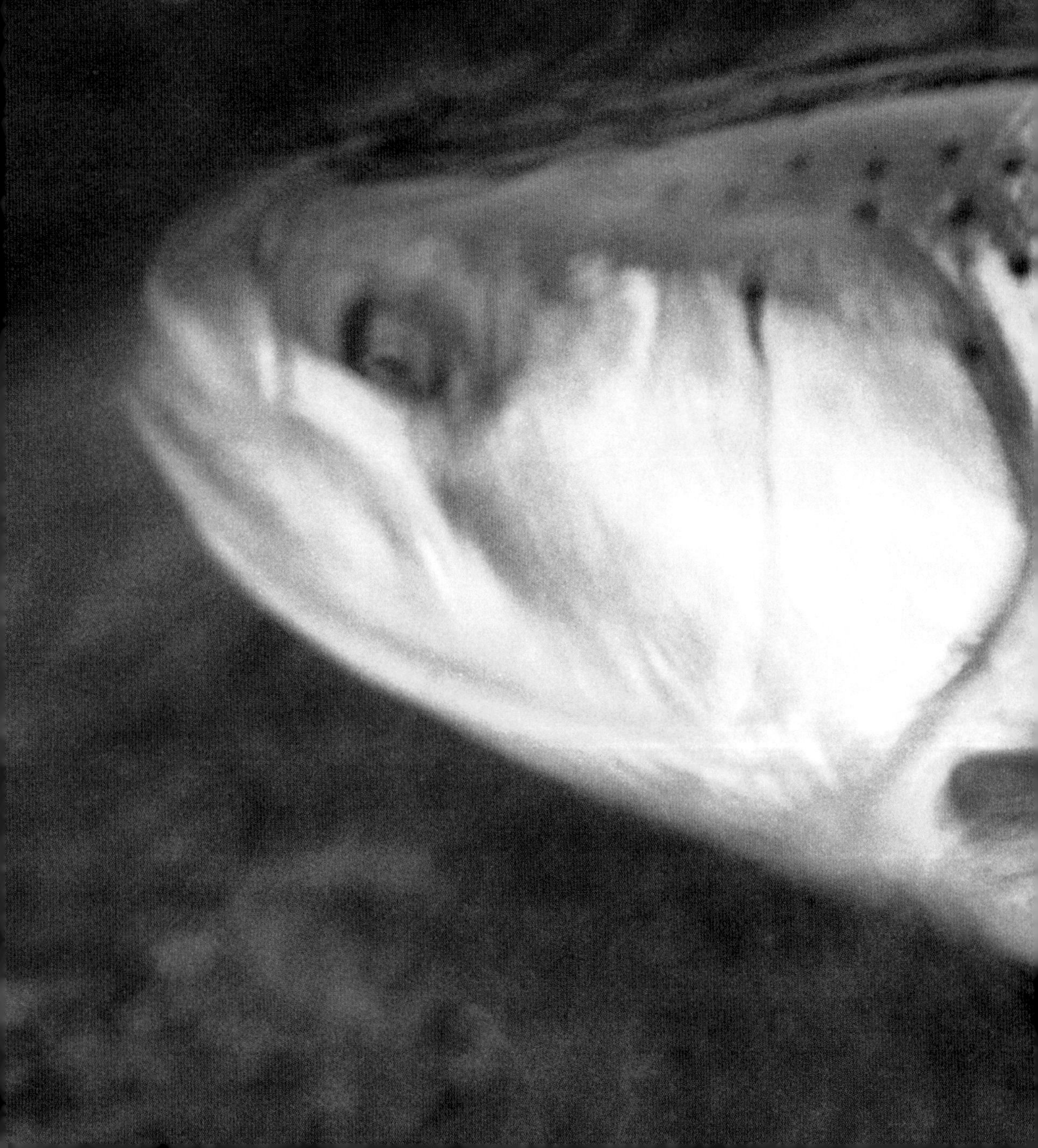

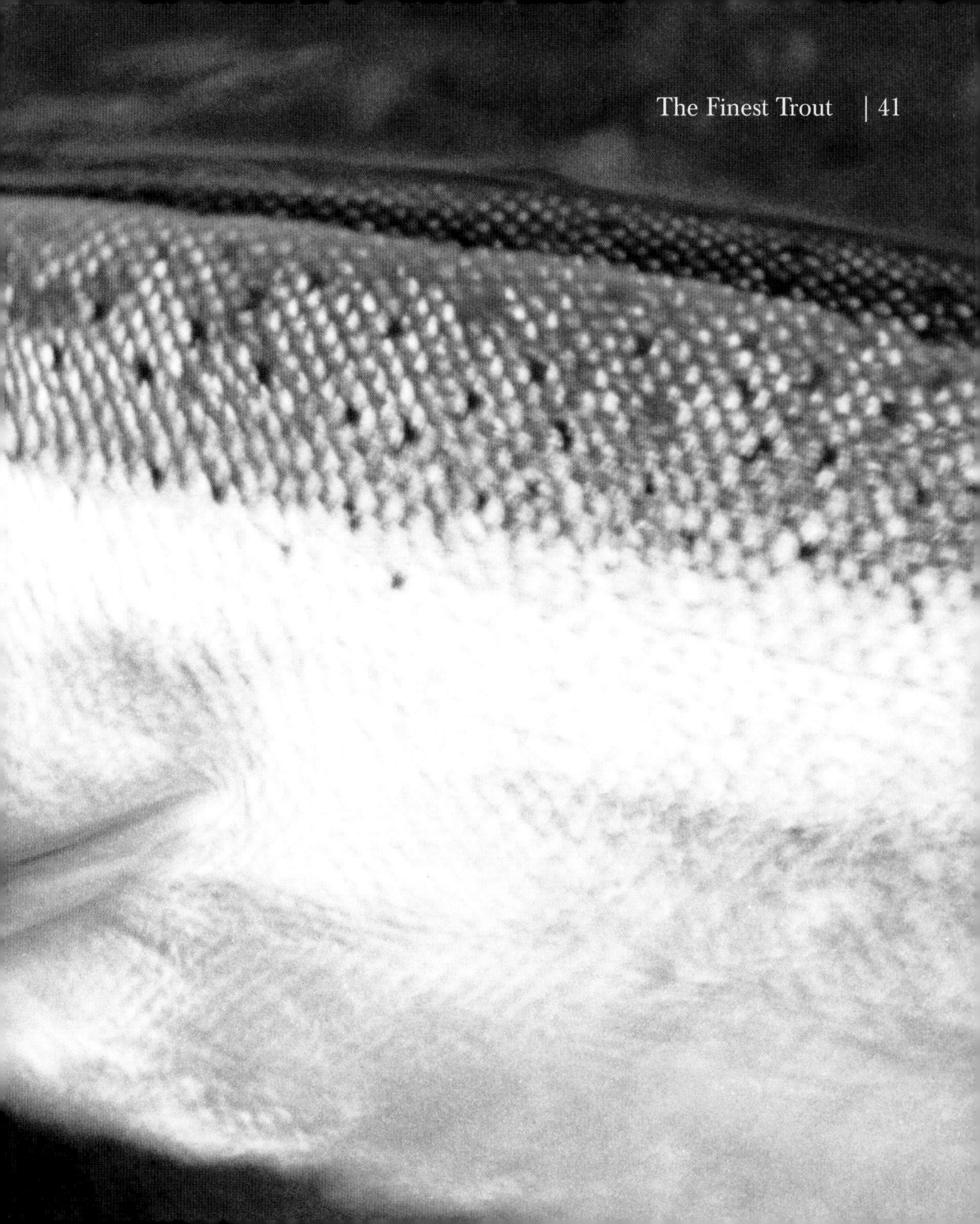

In the Steelhead's Eye

Through the window of the steelhead's eye

I have seen pictures of the infant soul of man

Prehistoric peoples proud, brave and holistic

At the mercy of a rugged, fecund land

Awestruck and respectful of providence.

I have seen European peoples

Driven great distances by the desire for freedom and money

Their colonizing manifest as divine domain and the Will of God

Seen them confounded and cross-purposed by magnificence of setting,

The need for sustenance and fear of the Other.

They imposed markets of extraction and consumption

In the name of Survival, then Prosperity

Then Comfort, then Progress for the Sake of Progress

Then Progress for the Sake of More Progress

And then Progress Forgetting from Where and Why it Came.

They were attracted and challenged by the remoteness

Willful to change the face of the land

To redirect it, repurpose it – thinking it boundlessly elastic

Unaware of what was being erased forever

Unknowing what would be lost to those to come in spirit and well-being.

In the steelhead's eye I swear I have seen these things –

The collective and eternal map of DNA

The infinite natural jigsaw

A god-seed planted in the explosion of the universe

And life forming as the earth hurtled from the sun.

I see my fish emblematic

A fuzzy legend of cold waters swift and sweet. A noble icon of survival

Yielding just enough to give us something of ourselves to see

Robust and individual, whimsical, a desirable object

Immaculately designed for the life it lives.

I see in the steelhead a Western Moby

A mirror for the Great Northwest. A pan-cultural totem

Symbolizing myriad destinies of peoples and place

An organism with the ecological wisdom of 100 centuries

Swimming in the shadows of all who have gone before.

It is, like the place –

A wild prize that can be grasped but not won

A force that can be harnessed but not subdued

A dream that can be sold but never owned

To tame it would be to kill it.

At the End of a Thin Line

I made gifts to the steelhead

Articles of feathers and fur

Some rich, colorful and gaudy

Some muted, restrained and respectful of the river's camouflage

All hope and speculation against tall odds.

Largely they have been denied

Bobbing in the current threads like overdressed beggars

But enough times folly has given way to luck

The right time has passed reasonably close to the right place

And at the end of a thin line I have felt a vibrant force of life.

Enough times I have been jolted alive

By the savage suddenness of the strike

By the astonishing speed of the steelhead's run

By the spectacular display when the fish leaps – an aerodynamic wonder

Vaulting high above the river's surface in a glittering spray.

In such moments I have been dissolved

Often for but a fleeting, flickering instant

Occasionally for long enough to saturate my consciousness

With the guilty pleasure of capture and inspection, revival and release

Always I am enriched, humbled and wiser for the experience.

Always I am reminded of the rich and dense fabric of life

Of the complexities of the natural world

The intangible and inspirational worth of wildness

The insignificance and importance of every detail

And of the tireless beauty of what was and what has yet to come.

Always I am filled with a strange lust and yearning for ideas invisible

For the missing piece in a riddle where neat answers do not exist

For the sequence to happen again and again so I can pay closer attention

To see more clearly what it is I saw

And feel more intensely what it is I felt.

A Daunting Tangle

In the pastoral world of angling lurks paradox and problem

Waits interception, circumvention, foil and deceit

We strive to know the river. To understand the struggle subsurface

We seek a oneness with seasons and cycles, events and patterns

Yet we know, in success, we intrude.

It is cruel that a singular being's life should be so interrupted

But *heinous* that the fate of an entire species fall captive to apathy

That a millenniums-old pulse of life be trumped

Stymied by a roughshod way that does not recognize its responsibility

By a culturally-sanctioned, corporate indifference.

It is impossibly cruel that humanity faces such a dilemma

Knowing that civilization is essential for survival

That we extract from the earth food, water, comfort and convenience

– And give back a vastness of waste. That every civilized bite we take

Yields a moral cipher and a daunting tangle.

Perhaps it is a hypocritical and harmful subterfuge

That a compassionate and rational person goes fishing for sport

Or perhaps, it is an innately nostalgic act. A search for ancient meanings

For prehistoric relationships. An attempt to find our place

Perhaps it is merely recreational escape.

Angling might be all or none of those things

In practice it may hardly matter

But it is a fruit of complex flavor that can be slowly eaten and savored –

Layers of intoxication, improbability, endurance and disappointment

Giving way to a sweet marrow of fulfillment and new challenge.

It is a path like the steelhead's journey

An adventure into an ocean of uncertainty and richness

A siren that pulls us back to moving water

To the cradle of wilderness life. To birth. To a symbolic place

Where humanity must reconcile the value of what is wild.

And if in this tangle we are fortunate and smart

If we collectively pay heed to the signs we are given

If we allow the river and our thoughts to run free

If with the murmuring cadence we cooperate rather than dominate

We may find a way to truth and purpose.

We may find in the river a gleaming prize

A litmus for the health of the very elements that sustain us

We may find in the river our own silver revelations

Shining fragments in the web of life

We may find in the river, steelhead.

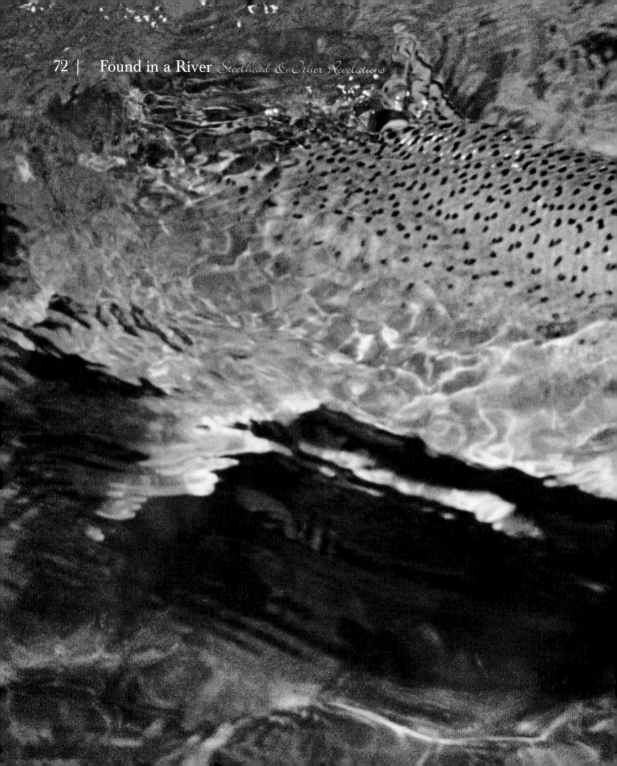